THE DINOSAUR IS THE BIGGEST ANIMAL THAT EVER LIVED

AND OTHER WRONG IDEAS YOU THOUGHT WERE TRUE

BY SEYMOUR SIMON
ILLUSTRATED BY GIULIO MAESTRO

J.B. Lippincott   New York

11,396

Library of Congress Cataloging in Publication Data
Simon, Seymour.
    The dinosaur is the biggest animal that ever lived,
and other wrong ideas you thought were true.

    Summary: Explains why many commonly accepted
scientific "facts"—lightning never strikes twice, the
sky is blue, snakes are slimy, etc.—are untrue.
    1. Science—Juvenile literature. [1. Science—
Miscellenea] I. Maestro, Giulio, ill. II. Title.
Q163.S497 1984   500   83-48960
ISBN 0-397-32075-2
ISBN 0-397-32076-0 (lib. bdg.)

CONTENTS

INTRODUCTION

Snakes are slimy. The sky is blue. The dinosaur is the biggest animal that ever lived. A compass needle points to the North Pole. Chocolate causes pimples. How many of these sayings do you believe are true? Would you believe that none of them is true?

In this book, we'll look at some common ideas and sayings about people, animals, the world around you, and space. You'll find out the reasons why the sayings are all wrong and why you shouldn't believe everything you hear. You may also find out that in many cases truth is stranger than fiction.

THE DINOSAUR IS THE BIGGEST
ANIMAL THAT EVER LIVED

The largest dinosaur may have been 100 feet long and weighed over 80 tons. Its name is "Ultrasaurus." The bone that made up its shoulder blade was nearly nine feet long. This huge animal lived 140 million years ago. It was the largest *land* animal ever to walk the Earth.

But this giant dinosaur was smaller than an animal that is still alive today, the blue whale. The largest blue whales are over 100 feet long and weigh more than 160 tons!

Even a baby blue whale is large. A newborn blue whale may be over 25 feet long and weigh three tons. In a year's time, the young blue whale may weigh more than 25 tons.

Hundreds of thousands of blue whales have been killed by whalers since the beginning of the century. It is a shame that these magnificent animals have been hunted and killed in such numbers. Countries belonging to the International Whaling Commission have banned all members from catching the blue whale. Perhaps the blue whale will not disappear along with the dinosaur, at least not in our time.

LIGHTNING NEVER
STRIKES TWICE

Despite the old saying that lightning never
strikes twice in the same place, lightning can
and does. For example, the top of the Empire
State Building has been struck a dozen times

within the space of a few minutes. Tall buildings, TV antennas, and trees are often struck
repeatedly during thunderstorms.

Lightning is a giant spark of electricity in
the atmosphere. Lightning can leap from one

cloud to another or from a cloud to the ground or from the ground to a cloud. Thunder is the sound of lightning. The flash heats the air around it. The sound is caused when air expands suddenly and then cools and contracts rapidly. The little snap you get from an electric spark is a kind of tiny thunder.

There may be more lightning around than you think. Weather scientists say that there are 1,800 thunderstorms going on around Earth at any one time. They figure that lightning is striking the ground around the world an average of 100 times each second.

THE SUN IS FARTHEST FROM EARTH IN WINTER

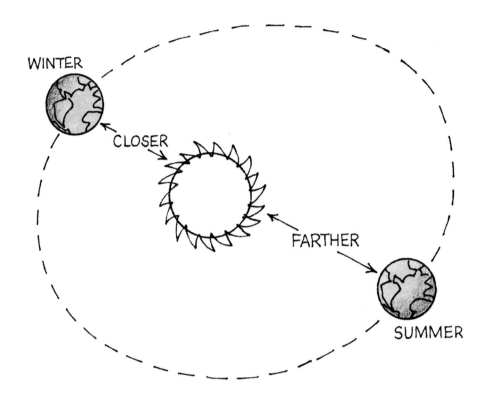

Many people think it is cold in winter because the sun is farthest from Earth at that time. As a matter of fact, the reverse is true. Earth is closest to the sun in December and farthest from the sun in early July. The difference is about three million miles. That does have a slight effect on temperatures on Earth, but it does not cause seasons.

Seasons are caused by the tilt of Earth's axis, about 23½ degrees. For part of each year, the northern half of Earth is tilted toward the sun. The sun's rays strike Earth straighter in the northern half, giving it summer. The southern half of Earth is tilted away from the sun, and it has winter.

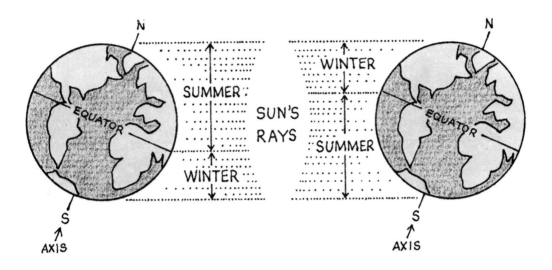

As Earth travels in its orbit around the sun, the northern half tilts away and the southern half tilts toward the sun. The seasons change. It is winter in the northern half and summer in the southern half. There would be no seasons as we know them if Earth were straight up in space.

11

THE OCTOPUS CAN SQUEEZE
A PERSON TO DEATH

The many stories of octopuses holding divers or even boats in a viselike grip are just fiction. An octopus never strangles or crushes a victim with its tentacles. The tentacles are used just to hold an animal so that the octopus can bite with its parrotlike beak. Many octopuses are slightly poisonous, but only the venom of the blue-ringed octopus of the South Pacific can be deadly to humans.

Most octopuses are small. Some are only a few inches across. But even the biggest kinds seldom harm people. Octopuses are usually

shy and will hide in the cracks between underwater rocks. If poked by a diver, an octopus will give off a cloud of ink and try to escape instead of attacking.

Once in a while, a swimmer will be held by the suckers of an octopus's tentacles. Divers say that a firm grip on an octopus's head and body is enough to make it relax its hold. Even when the octopus bites, it usually results in only a slight swelling.

IT'S EASY TO IDENTIFY A POISONOUS MUSHROOM

There is no easy way to tell if a mushroom is poisonous or safe to eat. The idea that you can safely eat a mushroom if it is white or because it has a good smell is not correct. Some deadly poisonous mushrooms are white and smell fine. On the other hand, an edible mushroom can turn brown, blue, red, purple, and even black and still be safe. And some very unpleasant-smelling mushrooms can be eaten with no ill effect.

Some "cooking hints" that supposedly make a mushroom safe to eat are also wrong. One incorrect idea is that cooking a poisonous mushroom in vinegar makes it safe. In fact, there is no easy way to make a poisonous mushroom safe to eat. Another incorrect idea is that a safe mushroom, unlike a poisonous one, can be peeled.

There is only one way that you can tell whether a mushroom is safe. That way is to identify the particular kind exactly by using an illustrated guide. The best advice is to eat only those mushrooms that are sold in food stores.

LEAD PENCILS CONTAIN LEAD

A lead pencil contains no lead at all. The "lead" is actually a strip of graphite, a little clay, and a little water. Graphite is a soft form of carbon, chemically the same as diamonds. Both are made of pure carbon, but while graphite is one of the softest of all minerals, diamond is the hardest. They differ only in the way their molecules are arranged.

Graphite is black, feels greasy to the touch, and leaves a mark on paper. Graphite is ground up, mixed with clay and water, and baked. It is pushed into a mold that shapes it and then cut to the right lengths.

You might think that the graphite is then inserted into a thin hole in a wooden pencil. But that is not so. The graphite strips are actually placed in grooves cut in a flat slat of wood. A second grooved slat is placed over the first, and the two slats are glued together. Then the slats are run through machines that cut and facet them and divide them into individual pencils. Other machines add finishing touches such as paint and an eraser at one end.

LEMMINGS MARCH INTO THE SEA TO COMMIT SUICIDE

Every four years, the legend tells us, lemmings gather in the millions. Then the small Norwegian rodents begin to march down to the sea. When they arrive at the shore, they plunge into the water and commit suicide by drowning.

The only trouble with this legend is that it is not true. Lemmings don't commit suicide. Just like any other animal, they try to survive.

In the hills of Norway where they live, lemmings are usually scarce. But what apparently happens is that every four years or so their population explodes. The large numbers of lemmings overcrowd the countryside and eat all the available food.

Millions of the lemmings begin to move down the hills in their search for food and less crowded places. As they move, they often swim across small streams. Many die along the way, for they make easy prey and are in a weakened condition. Many others reach the ocean shore and plunge into the water, much the same as they do when they cross a stream. But they swim too far out to make it back, and the waves overwhelm them. The lemmings die in large numbers, but are not suicides. They die in an attempt to survive.

THE SKY IS BLUE

Sometimes the sky looks blue. But other times it looks gray or black, and at sunset or sunrise it may look orange or red. The air, which makes up the sky, has no color of its own. The colors are caused by what happens to light rays as they travel through the air.

The light from our sun looks white, but it is made up of all the colors of the rainbow: red, orange, yellow, green, blue, indigo, and violet. When sunlight passes through the lower atmosphere, its rays are scattered by tiny particles in the air. It's the scattered rays we see, the rays that are reflected to us by the particles. The blue rays are scattered more easily than the reds and yellows. That's why the sky most often seems to light up blue.

You can show how this happens by a simple demonstration. Stir a few drops of milk into a bottle of water. The tiny droplets of milk represent the particles in the atmosphere. Shine a flashlight against the side of the bottle. The milk particles scatter the light and reflect the blue rays so the mixture looks blue.

On the moon, where there is no air, the sky is always black even when the sun is shining. The sky also looks black to astronauts in the space shuttle because they are above almost all of the atmosphere.

THE INSIDES OF ALL PEOPLE ARE ALIKE

Models, charts, and books give us the idea that all people are alike inside. They show the stomach to be a certain size and in a certain place. They show the heart and the blood vessels to be exactly here or exactly there.

But these models and charts show an average person. Just as we don't expect everyone to have the same size arms or noses, we shouldn't expect everyone to have the same size hearts or stomachs.

People's insides can differ in many ways. For example, most adults have 206 bones, but infants have more bones than adults. As a child grows older, some of the bones fuse together so that the number of bones is reduced. Adults differ as well. Some people have four bones at the end of their backbone, but other people have five.

Stomachs, hearts, and other internal organs vary in shape, size, and position. Even the numbers of organs can be different. Most people have three arteries (a kind of blood vessel) branching off from the aorta (a main artery). But other people have as few as one or as many as six arteries branching off their aortas. People are as individual on the inside as they are on the outside.

THE LARGER THE BIRD,
THE BIGGER THE EGG

It sounds reasonable that a bigger bird will lay a bigger egg than a smaller bird. But that's not the way it is. The kiwi is a small bird that lays a large egg. The kiwi weighs about as much as a chicken—about four pounds. But the kiwi egg weighs one pound, one-fourth of its body weight.

The egg of the kiwi is larger in proportion to its body than the egg of any other bird in the world. An ostrich egg is only about three times heavier than a kiwi egg. But the ostrich is 75 times heavier than the kiwi. If an ostrich

24

egg were in the same proportion to the ostrich as the kiwi egg is to a kiwi, an ostrich egg would weigh 75 pounds.

The male kiwi sits on the egg until it hatches. The chick is born after 11 weeks,

almost a record for birds. The chick is covered with straggly feathers, and will grow into an adult after three or four years.

The kiwi is a native of New Zealand. It gets its name from the cry it makes when courting— a shrill whistle that sounds like "k-wee." It is one of the few birds that cannot fly.

A CAT'S EYES GLOW
IN THE DARK

A cat's eyes don't really glow. If a cat were in complete darkness, you couldn't see its eyes. But shine a light on a cat, and the light enters the cat's eyes and is reflected back so well that the eyes seem to glow.

Night animals such as cats, raccoons, and bullfrogs have something in their eyes that

help them to see in the dark. They have shiny, reflecting cells behind the retina of their eyes. The cells form a membrane called the tapetum. It acts like a mirror.

Some of the light entering a cat's eyes passes through the retina. The tapetum reflects the light back, giving it another chance to be absorbed. The tapetum is responsible for the pale green shine of a cat's eyes, the yellow of a raccoon's eyes, and the cloudy green of a bullfrog's eyes.

Cats' eyes look different at night than they do during the day. At night their pupils look wide and round. In the bright light of day, they narrow to slits. The pupils have two sides that open and close like sliding curtains. In the dark they are wide open, but in bright light they close down.

QUICKSAND DRAGS
A PERSON UNDER

Many stories are told about people who take one false step into quicksand and are pulled under. The stories are true mostly in the imagination of the writer. Quicksand, sometimes called running sand, does exist. But quicksand does not pull anyone down under its surface. And getting stuck in quicksand is not an automatic death sentence.

Quicksand is a bed of loose sand and water, usually found at the mouths of rivers where drainage is poor. The water makes the smooth, rounded grains of sand very slippery and unstable.

But if you can float on water, then you can easily float on quicksand. Quicksand is about twice as buoyant as water. If you are caught in quicksand, the important thing is not to struggle. If you thrash around trying to get out, you'll only push your body deeper. But it isn't the quicksand that is pulling you under, it's your struggles that are pushing you under.

The way to get out of quicksand is to remain calm and lie on your back. Just as you would float in water, you will be supported by the quicksand. Then slowly push or pull your body toward firm land.

A COMPASS NEEDLE POINTS
TO THE NORTH POLE

If you keep following a compass needle to get to the North Pole, you will never get there. A compass needle doesn't point to true north. It actually points to the *magnetic* north pole, which is about 11 degrees away from true north, 90 degrees. Using a compass you would end up near Prince of Wales Island, about 700 miles from the North Pole.

It is true that Earth is like a large magnet. But its lines of magnetic force are irregular. The difference between true north and a compass reading is called the magnetic declination. Not only does a compass not point to the true North Pole, but the declination varies at different places on Earth.

The magnetic poles do not even remain in the same place all the time. They are continually wandering around. So the declination keeps changing as the poles keep moving. Finally and most surprising is the fact that magnetic north and south have changed position many times in the past. If you went back in time a few million years, your compass would point south instead of north.

HOT WATER CRACKS A THIN GLASS MORE EASILY THAN A THICK ONE

If you pour hot water (or any other hot liquid) into a thick glass it is likely to crack. On the other hand, hot water is not as likely to crack a thin glass. That's true even though thick glass is stronger than thin glass.

Here's the reason. Like most materials, glass expands when it is heated. When you pour a hot liquid into a thick glass, the inside of the glass near the heat expands. But glass is a poor conductor of heat. So the outside of the glass does not heat up and expand as quickly.

The difference between the rates at which the inside and outside expand causes a

32

strain on the glass. The strain is often strong enough to crack the glass.

But when you pour hot water into a thin glass, the heat reaches the outside much more quickly. Both the inside and the outside of the glass expand at the same rate. There is no strain, and the glass is not as likely to crack. That's one reason why test tubes and other laboratory glassware are made of thin glass.

By the way, you can help to prevent a thick glass from cracking by warming both the outside and the inside before you fill it with a hot liquid.

YOU CAN'T GET SUNBURNED ON A CLOUDY DAY

A sunburn is an injury to your skin. A bad sunburn causes your skin to react exactly as it would to any other kind of burn. A sunburn is caused by the invisible ultraviolet rays of the sun. Thin clouds do not filter out ultraviolet rays. So you can get a sunburn on a cloudy day.

Here's what happens when you get sunburned. The sun's rays cause the tiny blood vessels in your skin to open wider, increasing the flow of blood in them. That's what makes your skin red. The blood also makes the walls of the blood vessels more likely to break. At the same time, the ultraviolet rays cause the skin to release chemicals that make the skin swell and blister. A bad sunburn can last for two weeks.

Tanning the skin is not the same as burning the skin. A tan is the result of a substance in the skin called melanin. The melanin in the skin increases and is spread around when the skin is exposed to ultraviolet rays. That helps to protect the skin against damage by the rays. Some people have enough melanin to look dark at all times. Other people do not have enough melanin to tan at all. The less melanin in your skin, the easier it is to get a painful sunburn.

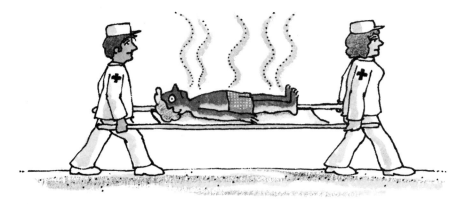

YOU CAN SEE A MILLION STARS
ON A CLEAR NIGHT

The stars seem to fill the sky on a clear night. Their numbers seem countless. You may be surprised to find out that a person with good eyesight can see only about 2,000 stars without a telescope. If you live in a brightly-lit city, you can see far fewer than 2,000.

Of course, there are many more stars in the universe than that. Our galaxy, called the Milky Way galaxy, contains about 100 billion stars. But we don't live in the center of the Milky Way where the stars are thickly clustered. Our sun and solar system are on the outskirts of the galaxy, out in the suburbs, you might say. Here the stars are fewer and farther apart.

Each star is a sun and is very bright. But most of the stars in our galaxy are so far away that we cannot see them with our unaided eyes. You are also viewing the stars through miles and miles of Earth's atmosphere. The atmosphere contains water, dust, smoke, and other particles that make it difficult to see the stars clearly.

Most stars in the universe are so far away we can't see them even with the most powerful telescope on Earth.

BACTERIA ARE BAD

Some kinds of bacteria do cause disease, and these are certainly harmful. But many kinds of bacteria are harmless. Other kinds of bacteria are useful. And still other kinds of bacteria are absolutely needed by living things. Saying bacteria are bad is like saying that people are bad. Some are and some aren't.

Without certain kinds of bacteria in your body, you could not digest food. Other bacteria take the gas nitrogen from the air and fix it in the soil so that it can be used by certain plants.

Bacteria are important in causing dead plant and animal parts to decay. Without death and decay there can be no new life. New plants and animals need the materials that decay puts back into the soil and air. These materials are never used up. Bacteria help to pass them on to each new living thing.

People use bacteria to make cheese, wine, vinegar, pickles, and other foods. Bacteria are also used to turn plant materials into alcohol, which can be used as a fuel. Many new uses for bacteria are just now being discovered.

MT. EVEREST IS THE TALLEST MOUNTAIN ON EARTH

Mt. Everest is not the tallest mountain, and the Himalayas are not the largest mountain range. The greatest mountains were not discovered until this century. They are not even visible from the suface. That's because the greatest mountains on Earth lie underwater.

The biggest mountain range in the world is in the Atlantic, Indian, and Pacific Oceans. It is called the Mid-Oceanic Ridge. It stretches from Iceland to the southern tip of Africa, where it curves into the Indian and Pacific Oceans—45,000 miles in all. For much of its length, the ridge is 500 miles wide. By contrast, the Himalayas are 1,600 miles long and 150 miles wide.

Many individual mountains in the Mid-Oceanic Ridge rise above the water to form islands. The crests of these mountains rise higher above the ocean floor than Mt. Everest rises above sea level.

The world's tallest mountain is Mauna Kea on the island of Hawaii. Its combined height below the water and above the water is more than 33,000 feet, nearly a mile taller than Mt. Everest.

SATURN IS THE ONLY PLANET WITH RINGS

The rings of Saturn were discovered hundreds of years ago. The rings are made of many, many particles of dust and ice. The rings are very wide, almost 200,000 miles across. But they are very thin, no more than half a mile thick.

For many years, scientists were puzzled as to why Saturn was the only planet with rings. Today, we know that it isn't. Uranus and Jupiter also have rings, and scientists would not be surprised if Neptune turned out to have rings too.

Uranus's rings were discovered by scientists in 1977. Using telescopes and other instruments on Earth, the scientists found a series of narrow rings around Uranus. There seem to be several narrow rings separated by wide gaps. They are much narrower than Saturn's rings and very thin. They are also very dark, the color of coal dust. No one knows why this is so. In fact, many questions about all of the planetary rings still remain to be answered.

Jupiter's ring was discovered in 1979 by *Voyager 1*. The ring surrounds Jupiter like a faint smoke ring. The ring is made up of tiny particles of dust no bigger than those in smoke. When the sun is shining directly behind them, the particles glimmer like specks of dust in a beam of light.

FOOD SPOILS IN AN OPEN TIN CAN

Many people think that you shouldn't put a half-empty tin can of food into the refrigerator. They think that you should empty the unused food into a glass or plastic container. The metal can, they say, will spoil the food.

But that's just not true. Food in an open tin can will spoil no faster than food in glass or plastic. Of course, you should keep the can covered and refrigerated to guard against the growth of bacteria. Food will keep just as well in its original can as in another container. Left uncovered and unrefrigerated, the food will rot just as fast in glass as in a can.

Acid foods, such as citrus juices, sometimes take on an unpleasant taste in a tin can. But that taste is not the taste of poison, and will not harm you.

Finally, a tin can is really made of steel with a small amount of tin. Tin is too expensive to use to make a whole can. A "tin" can is made from a sheet of rolled steel that is coated on both sides with tin to prevent rusting.

SNAKES ARE SLIMY

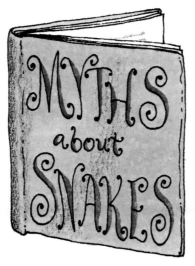 

There are more stories and myths about snakes than most other animals. Some of the stories are rarely heard these days, but others are still thought to be true.

For example, some people believe snakes are slimy. There is no truth to this. When out of water, a snake's skin is perfectly dry and cool to the touch. The snake's body is covered with hard, overlapping scales from the tip of its nose to the tip of its tail. The scales are like the shingles on a roof; they protect the snake from the outside world.

There is also no truth to the story that a mother snake swallows its young to protect them from danger. Even if a snake were to swallow its young, the baby would simply be digested in the mother's stomach. That's not great protection!

Another false idea is that snakes wait until sundown to die. Snakes die whenever they are killed. It is true, however, that a snake's muscles may continue twitching for some moments after death.

Here are some other wrong ideas about snakes: Horsehairs can turn into snakes. Snakes will not crawl over ropes. A snake

stays by the dead body of its mate hoping for revenge on the killer. All snakes are poisonous. None of these statements is true.

What is true about snakes is that they try to survive in the best ways they can. And like other animals, they form a part of the complex web of living things on Earth.

ANIMALS MOVE AROUND, PLANTS STAY STILL

Both of these statements are partly untrue. There are many kinds of animals that cannot move—at least at some stage in their lives. And there are many kinds of plants that can and do move.

For example, adult barnacles and adult coral animals remain firmly in place. Barnacles attach themselves to solid objects such as rocks and pilings. Their shell-like coverings become permanently attached to the surface. Coral animals usually live in large colonies that form tropical reefs and islands of coral rock.

Many clams and oysters are also unable to move when adults. While some kinds of clams can move short distances by means of a fleshy foot, thousands of other kinds remain anchored in place as adults.

There are many one-celled plants, on the other hand, that have no roots and can move. Some move by means of a long, thin tail that they whip through the water. This allows them to move a few feet per hour. That may not seem very fast, but compared to their size, it's about equal to a person running 100 miles an hour or faster.

Some larger plants, such as the Venus's-flytrap, can quickly move their leaves or other parts. The leaves of a Venus's-flytrap

are hinged down the middle. When an insect lands on a leaf, it triggers the leaf to fold together, trapping the insect inside. The whole action takes only a few seconds.

CHOCOLATE CAUSES PIMPLES

If you are not one of those unfortunate people who are allergic to chocolate, then it is unlikely that eating chocolate will give you skin problems. One study by skin doctors seems to show that chocolate has no effect on the skin one way or another. When people with acne were fed chocolate bars, most stayed the same while a few got better and a few got worse.

There are a lot of other myths about chocolate. For example, chocolate is not as fattening as many people think. Of course, it depends on how much you eat. But a cup of hot cocoa has fewer than 100 calories. A small amount of chocolate could probably fit into almost any diet.

Another untrue idea is that chocolate contains only "empty calories" and no real food value. In fact, chocolate is a good source of a number of minerals including calcium, phosphorus, and iron. A chocolate bar is also a good source of energy.

About the worst thing that you can say about chocolate is that it is not very good for your teeth. The chocolate allows decay-causing bacteria to grow in your mouth. However, the less time the chocolate stays in your mouth, the less harmful it is. And brushing your teeth after you eat chocolate (or any other sweet food) will help prevent tooth decay.

THERE IS ONE FULL MOON EACH MONTH

There can be zero, one, or two full moons each month. It all depends upon the month.

It takes just a little more than 29½ days for the moon to go through its phases, from one full moon to the next full moon. That means that in some months you can have a full moon on the first and also on the thirtieth or thirty-first. But the month of February is only 28 or 29 days long, shorter than a complete cycle of the moon. So about once every six years there is a February with no full moon.

The moon revolves around Earth from west to east. But because of Earth's rotation on its axis, the moon, like the sun and the stars, appears to rise from the east and set toward the west. The result of Earth's rotation and the moon's revolution is that the moon rises and sets about fifty minutes later each day.

Many early people based their yearly calendar on the month (or moonth). The Romans, for example, had 12 months of 30 and 29 days. This didn't work exactly, so they threw in an odd day, making a total of 355 days a year. Every other year they inserted another month, and every 24 years the calendar was readjusted. This was so complicated that you can see why we no longer base our calendar on the phases of the moon.

THERE ARE ONLY A FEW EARTHQUAKES EACH YEAR

There are over one million earthquakes every year, an average of two a minute. Most of the quakes are very mild, something like the shaking you might feel if a heavy truck rumbled by your home. Others, of course, are very strong, destroying buildings and killing hundreds or thousands of people.

Some places have far more earthquakes than others. There are two major earthquake zones around the world. One, called the Alptide Belt, stretches across Italy, Greece, Turkey, through the Middle East, and into Asia.

The other, called the Pacific Ring of Fire, rings the Pacific Ocean. California, Alaska, the islands of Japan, and the western coast of South America are in the Pacific Ring of Fire.

But earthquakes occur in many other places around the world. Each year, an average of 700 quakes hit the United States. About half of these are in southern California. The rest are scattered over most of the country, including New England, Missouri, and South Carolina. In fact, the only places in the United States where no earthquakes have ever been recorded are the southern half of Florida, the lower third of Alabama, and the lower half of Texas.

SHARKS ONLY ATTACK
IN DEEP WATER

Sharks, like snakes, are the subject of many stories and myths. Most of the stories are not true. For example, some people say that a shark will only attack a person in water ten feet or more deep. But sharks are known to have attacked people in knee-deep water. And even a freshly caught shark, high and dry on the deck of a boat or on shore, can bite off a leg or an arm that gets too close.

It is also said by some people that sharks need warm water in which to attack; that they have to roll over on their backs to bite; that they will not attack at night or if it is raining;

that they always swim with their fins showing above the water. All of these ideas are false.

Sharks can attack in any water, including the ice-cold waters of the Arctic. A shark can attack from its normal swimming position; they are easily able to get their jaws into position for biting. Sharks attack in daylight or at night, and in any kind of weather.

Sharks swim at different depths below the surface. Deep-swimming sharks do not have their fins showing. Many people have been attacked without any warning and with no fins showing in the area.

Not all sharks are dangerous. Most are harmless and will try to avoid people. The whale shark, the largest shark in the world, is quite harmless to people. It eats tiny sea animals and plants called plankton rather than flesh.

READING IN BED CAN RUIN YOUR EYES

Neither reading in bed nor reading in a moving car nor reading in a poor light can damage your eyes. All of these *can* cause you to strain your eye muscles and make them tired. They may even give you a headache. But they do not cause any lasting harm.

The reason your eyes may get tired if you read in bed is because of the position of your body. Your eye muscles become strained from trying to adjust to see at a difficult angle. But if you sit up straight in bed when you read, then you should have no difficulty.

Reading in a moving car or in poor light also cause muscle problems. But so do some kinds of fluorescent lighting, incorrect glasses or the lack of needed glasses, reading small print, and even watching a lot of TV.

These present no great problem for your eyes, however. All you have to do is rest your eyes from time to time and they will feel better. Poor vision is a result of a defect in the way your eyes work. Poor lighting does not cause the defect nor will good lighting prevent it.

PIGS ARE DIRTY AND STUPID

Pigs are neither dirty nor stupid. Pigs got the reputation of being dirty because they were usually kept in dirty pens. But pigs in the wild are no dirtier than any other forest animal.

It is true that on a hot day pigs like to wallow in mud. But that's for a good reason, not because they like dirt. Pigs can't perspire. The wet mud allows them to cool their bodies.

As for pigs being stupid, ask any farmer about that. Pigs often are able to open gates that other animals cannot. Pigs rank pretty high on the scale of animal intelligence— higher than dogs, cats, horses, or sheep.

In early times, pigs were used by English sportsmen to retrieve birds brought down in hunting. Europeans use pigs to hunt for a special kind of plant called a truffle.

When someone eats too much people say that he or she is "eating like a pig." That's very unfair. Pigs will eat only as much as they need to satisfy their hunger. Cows and horses are much more likely to overeat. Maybe we should say that sensible eaters "eat like pigs."

SHOOTING STARS ARE STARS

Shooting stars are not stars, nor do they shoot. "Shooting stars" is the name some people give to meteors. A meteor looks like a bright streak of light flashing across the night sky. But a meteor is not a star. Stars are suns far out in space. Meteors are bits of metal or rock burning up in Earth's atmosphere.

Meteoroids travel around the sun in orbits. We cannot see most of them because they are small and dark. Sometimes a meteoroid speeds into Earth's atmosphere. Then the meteoroid becomes red-hot and begins to glow. They are then called meteors. We see their bright flash for only a few seconds.

If a meteor is very large, it may not burn up completely in the atmosphere. It makes a bright streak across the sky and then falls to Earth's surface. A meteor that reaches the surface is called a meteorite.

Several thousand meteorites have been collected and examined by scientists. Most are just a few inches across, but some are very large. The American Museum of Natural History in New York City has a meteorite on display that weighs 31 tons. It fell thousands of years ago in Greenland and was brought to the museum in 1906.

What are your chances of being hit by a meteorite? Not very great, scientists say. Only about 150 meteorites a year land on the Earth. Yet a four-pound meteorite tore through the roof of a house in Wetherfield, Connecticut, on November 8, 1982. And only 11 years earlier, on April 8, 1971, another meteorite hit the roof of a house in Wetherfield less than a mile away.

Seymour Simon was born in New York City. He received his B.A. degree from City College, New York, and did graduate work there. He was a science teacher for a number of years and is now writing and editing full time.

Mr. Simon is the author of dozens of highly acclaimed science books for young readers, including KILLER WHALES; HOW TO BE A SPACE SCIENTIST IN YOUR OWN HOME; BODY SENSE, BODY NONSENSE; and COMPUTER SENSE, COMPUTER NONSENSE. More than thirty of his books have been selected as Outstanding Science Trade Books for Children by the National Science Teachers Association. He lives with his wife and two sons in Great Neck, New York.

Giulio Maestro was born in New York City and studied at the Cooper Union Art School and the Pratt Graphics Center. He has illustrated many popular books for children, including several written by his wife, Betsy, a kindergarten teacher. In addition to his picture-book illustration, Mr. Maestro is well known for his beautiful hand-lettering and his book jacket designs. He lives in Madison, Connecticut.

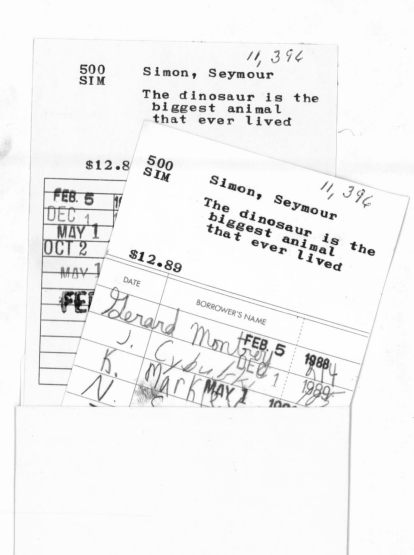

11,394

500
SIM

Simon, Seymour

The dinosaur is the
biggest animal
that ever lived

$12.8

FEB. 5	1
DEC 1	
MAY 1	
OCT 2	
MAY 1	
FE	

11,394

500
SIM

Simon, Seymour

The dinosaur is the
biggest animal
that ever lived

$12.89

DATE	BORROWER'S NAME		
Gerard	Mon	FEB. 5	1988
J.	Cybulsk	DEC 1	1984
K.	Mark	MAY 1	1989
N.			